ENGLISH
COUNTRY LIFE

ENGLISH COUNTRY LIFE

PB

PARKGATE
BOOKS

First Published in Great Britain in 1997
by Parkgate Books Ltd, London House, Great Eastern Wharf,
London SW11 4NQ

British Library Cataloguing in Publication Data:
A CIP catalogue record for this book is available from the
British Library.

ISBN 1 - 85585 - 326 - 4
1 3 5 7 9 8 6 4 2
Compiled by Philippa Lewis
Designed by Bill Mason
Printed and bound in Great Britain by
Butler & Tanner Ltd, Frome and London

INTRODUCTION

*These pictures of English country life span exactly
100 years, from the earliest photographs taken by
William Grundy for his book 'English Views' in
1857 at the beginning of the book to those at the end,
taken for the magazine 'Picture Post', which charted
British life in such extraordinary detail between the
years 1938 and 1957.*

*The following pages show the daily round and the
special events of life in the English countryside during
that period: they show some ways of life that have
long since disappeared and some that have remained
almost unchanged.*

QUEEN VICTORIA'S ENGLAND

A turnpike gate outside Hereford, photographed shortly before it was demolished in the 1870s. Relics from the 17th century, turnpikes were originally set up to levy tolls in order to pay for the upkeep of the roads. The tollkeeper who collected the money would have lived in the little cottage to the left, the windows so designed that he could look out in each direction. For the countryman, coming into town with produce to sell, the cost of taking his waggon through the gate would have been a consideration. In some districts there was a gate every 6 or 8 miles, and this made travelling slow and expensive.

QUEEN VICTORIA'S ENGLAND

Scenes of apparent tranquillity showing English country life during the reign of Queen Victoria. It was soon to be the end of an era: at the beginning of the 19th century agriculture was by far the most important form of production, but by 1901, when the Queen died, it accounted for only 6% of the national economy.

VIEWS FROM THE 1850S

*Two scenes recorded by a very early
photographer named William Grundy, from a
collection entitled 'English Views'. The farmer
in a stovepipe hat standing proudly at the gate
to his farmhouse, and the blacksmith working
on his anvil while a friend sits watching at the
forge door, would have had to stay still for up
to a minute for the photographs to be taken, so
giving them a rather stiff air.*

VICTORIAN COUNTRY PORTRAITS

Country folk carefully posed by the photographers with some of their everyday tools and utensils. The Victorian camera captured in detail their working clothes and stout boots, which would have been hand made by the village bootmaker. Men were more likely to buy their clothes, of heavyweight wool and corduroy, from markets in the local towns, but women's and children's clothes were usually made at home, and endlessly cut down, altered and re-stitched to save money. Travelling pedlars still roamed the country with stocks of haberdashery so that cottage women could brighten up old clothes with ribbons and bows.

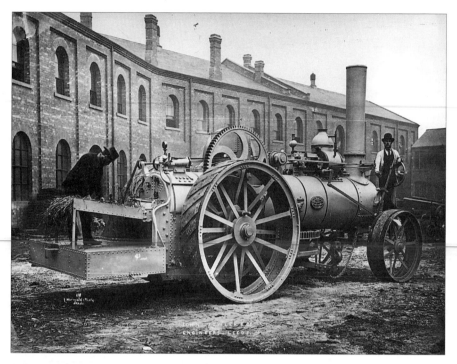

HORSEPOWER AND STEAMPOWER

*Although farmers continued to depend on horses to work
the land until the Second World War, the Victorian passion
for invention had given rise to many attempts to harness
steam power for the gruelling physical tasks of agriculture.
This steam ploughing engine of 1874 was designed to burn
straw. The problems with the new steam-powered machines
were many and various: agricultural labourers had to
learn new skills to operate them, and there was much loss
of life and limb as a result of such disasters as heavy
machinery overturning and boilers exploding. The massive
weight of the engines made them impractical for use on all
but the driest land, and they were slow to move from site
to site. It was not until the internal combustion engine was
adapted to agricultural use that mechanization was
introduced successfully.*

VILLAGE CHILDREN

*Sandringham in November 1925
and the children of the village are
photographed by a news agency
listening to one of the older
inhabitant's memories of Queen
Alexandra, who has just died. She
had married Edward VII in 1863
when he was Prince of Wales. The
estate at Sandringham was given to
the Prince by his father, Prince Albert,
and Edward and Alexandra were
devoted to the place. They made it the
centre of their family and social life,
using it for weekend house parties
and shooting parties.*

COUNTRY CHILDHOOD

Freedom to roam: children play on stepping stones in a quiet river near Meavy in Devon, and a farmer's daughter clutching a sheep's fleece leaps across the River Tyne in Northumberland.

VILLAGE SCHOOLS

Scenes in the village school: Parracombe in Devon (above) in 1954 and Lovington in Somerset (right) in 1948. These schoolrooms seem barely to have changed since they were built a century before. Education for every child became law only in 1870, and even then many children in rural areas did not attend regularly because they were needed to work in the fields. A typical village school had one room, with a partition to separate the infants from the older boys and girls.

HELPING OUT

A boy helps his father in the village bakery at Therfield in Hertfordshire, while lads take charge of a pony trap delivering milk in Todmorden in the West Riding and a donkey cart in St Ives. In 1918 the school leaving age was raised to fourteen; both before and after this many country children, in families that depended on their help, were expected to work after school hours.

SIMPLE PLEASURES

*Children cluster round a balloon-seller in the Market
Square in Richmond, Yorkshire, in the 1920s, while twenty
years later children search for bargains on a Red Cross
stall in wartime Devon.*

CHILDHOOD GAMES

*A contrast in styles: three-year-old Master
Lawson keeping dry at a gymkhana in Epsom,
Surrey, in 1934, while posing for the camera
and being held firmly on the leading rein. In
1938 the 'Picture Post' photographer took this
group of children playing on a wall at the edge
of the Cornish village of St Ives.*

THE HEART OF THE VILLAGE

Church spires and towers have dominated the rural landscape of England since medieval times: constant features in an ever-changing landscape. These views of Parracombe in Devon (right) and Ambleside in the Lake District (above) show occupations that also stayed the same with the passing centuries – a woman working in the sunlight at a cottage door and men labouring to bring in the hay. However a warning note was sounded in the caption to the Devon photograph, taken in 1954, that Britain was losing a farm every day.

THE CHURCH

The parson was traditionally one of the leaders of the village and responsible for the welfare of his parishioners. He was also regarded as a man of learning and often taught in the village school, particularly if it was affiliated to the church. The upkeep of the church itself was the responsibility of the parson, and hence his leadership in matters of fundraising. Otherwise his duties lay in christening, marrying and burying his flock, and conducting the regular church services. At Busbridge church, near Godalming (above), local people gather in 1933 to watch the wedding of Miss Isabel Buzzard to Lieutenant Herbert Acworth. The Sunday service (left) is taking place in Lovington, Somerset, in 1948.

THE VILLAGE STREET

Two old men sit peacefully in the sun
on the village green at East Witton
near Jervaulx, in Yorkshire.
The date is 1955 and there is
not a car in sight.

SHOPS AND SHOPPING

*In the 19th century villages were almost entirely self-sufficient:
people grew their own produce and bought whatever else they
needed from local craftsmen and itinerant traders. However, at
the turn of the century village shops became far more common, as
factory-made goods grew in availability and quality. The goods
were extensively advertised, and enamelled signs supplied by the
manufacturers appeared even in remote areas. Bakeries and
post offices, drapers, grocers and butchers opened
in the smallest villages. Kelly's directory for 1895, for example,
lists two shopkeepers in the village of Brixton Deverill in
Wiltshire, which had a population of only 112. The tradition of
mobile trade continued, as shown by this hardware salesman in a
small village in Devon.*

COUNTRY COTTAGES

Many villagers did not own their cottages but were tenants of the local squire or farmer, in whose hands lay responsibility for the condition of the buildings. By the early 20th century many ancient cottages were in a state of dereliction and had often simply been left to fall down. This was partly because, with the increase in mechanical farm implements, there was less work for agricultural labourers, and many had to move to towns and cities to find employment. Lord Curzon wrote in a letter to 'Country Life', 'It would be a national tragedy if these old buildings were to be replaced by a new standardized cottage, dumped down either singly or – still worse – in rows like a lot of band-boxes or dog-kennels.' In fact many of the cottages were rented or bought by 'new' country dwellers, either commuters or weekenders. In 1927 it was reported, 'Thirty years ago all these cottages belonged to the agricultural labourers, who paid from fifteen pence to two shillings a week rent; today, where they are rented, they fetch from £20 to £30 a year.'

THE MILL

The miller was an important figure in the rural community, grinding the corn for farmers and smallholders as and when it was needed. His was one of the most ancient of trades, the earliest windmill in England being recorded just after 1180. By the end of 19th century local windmills were being put out of business by the large urban powered mills, and wheat and flour were being imported from abroad. The photograph shows Four Swift Windmill in Sussex, described at the time as the oldest windmill in the county. In England in 1851 there were 37,000 millers, but their numbers were soon to decline. These millers, photographed in the mid-20th century, document the end of an era.

VILLAGE INSTITUTIONS

Photographs from the early 1950s showing the interiors of the pub and the village shop, both institutions at the heart of the community, with fixtures and fittings apparently unchanged since the previous century. The pub in the mining village of Eastwood in Derbyshire has the traditional games of cribbage, dominoes and solitaire on the table. The Hampshire shopkeeper holds a ration book and offers a chair to a tired customer.

THE PUB

Village pubs had stayed almost the same for hundreds of years, usually two or three to a village, and sometimes more. There was often a beer cellar as well, where ale could be bought but not consumed on the premises. The drinkers were nearly all men, and traditionally pubs were the only places where such controversial subjects as politics and religion could be discussed. The furnishings were very simple: wooden benches and tables with games supplied by the landlord to help swell the number of customers. The games were in some cases as ancient as the pubs themselves: skittles had originated in the 14th century; shove-halfpenny, as is being played in this pub in the West Country, had been known since the end of the 18th century. Later, a new kind of country pub began to appear, aimed at the passing trade of motorist, caravanner or hiker. With a well-furnished saloon bar, it was a place that women could enter without feeling uncomfortable. This bar above in the Pennines was photographed in 1947.

WATER AND WASHING

*Far into the 20th century many houses and cottages were
still without piped water. As late as 1946 a survey of
Gloucestershire showed that only 62% of the county's 292
parishes had piped supplies, and some of these only
amounted to public taps or standpipes in the street, as
photographed in 1938. The men taking a break,
photographed in the same year, have been hauling timber
with a team of horses, their astonishingly muddy clothes a
testament to the type of work involved.*

COUNTRY CRAFTS

*Many country women made a crucial
contribution to the family income by
working at home. Traditional
women's crafts included straw-
plaiting, knitting, glove-making and
lace-making. Children often helped
too. Whenever possible people worked
outside in order to get a good light,
because of course there was no electric
light. These women, photographed in
Coggeshall, Essex, in 1913, are
making tambour lace, the patterns
embroidered onto a net background.
Pillow or bobbin lace was finer and
more difficult to work: it took about
12 hours to make a yard of lace as
wide as a fingernail and was a
speciality of some areas of Devon and
Buckinghamshire.*

RURAL INDUSTRIES

*Many country industries depended on local
materials – clay for the pottery made at
Verwood in Dorset and withies that grew on
the banks of the Severn for the baskets and
fish traps in these pictures. The skills
involved were usually handed down from
one generation to the next.*

WHEELS AND WAGGONS

The last wheelwrights: George Huffey of Ingatestone in Essex photographed with a newly-built farm waggon in May 1947. The waggon was to be pulled by heavy horses and used for the hay harvest that summer (though it cannot have been a matter of more than a few years before it was replaced by a tractor and trailer). The wheelwright was important to the rural community, for every single cart, waggon, plough, roller, barrow, dray and carriage had need of the wheels that he made by hand. He had to judge the right strength, size and weight for each individual job, and one Victorian wheelwright described how he took into account the nature of the soil on the customer's farm and the temper of his horses.

THE WORKSHOP

Two country workshops in the early 1950s:
Mr Fuller, a saddler and ropemaker of
Urchfont in Wiltshire, and Mr Raven, a
sailmaker of Maldon in Essex. Both of their
skills, unlike those of the wheelwright, could
be adapted to the needs of the later 20th
century, the saddler making saddles and
bridles for the growing band of leisure horse
and pony riders, and the sailmaker moving
from work on the traditional East coast
barges to yachts.

TIME OFF

Summer cricket and winter skating: a cricket match in the grounds of Penshurst Castle, Kent, in the summer of 1935, and skating on a Wiltshire lake one winter in the 1930s. The cricket team was a unifying element in the village, the players coming from all walks of life. The mythical strength of the blacksmith was the mainstay of the team and competition with local villages fierce. The whole neighbourhood took an interest and turned out to watch the matches: few farmers would have risked the disapproval of the village by refusing their men time off to play.

SUMMER FESTIVITIES

*Under garlands of roses the children
of Denham in Buckinghamshire
process through the village street at
the Village Fair in 1925.
Some of the children's costumes
suggest a Regency theme.*

HIKING HOLIDAYS

*There was no law establishing the right to a
paid holiday until 1938 and prior to that
many people simply took days out in the
country, like these hikers setting off from
Euston Station in 1935. The Youth Hostel
Association of Great Britain was formed in
1930, 'to help all, especially young people
of limited means, to a greater knowledge,
love and care of the countryside,
particularly by providing simple
accommodation for them in their travels.'
The group setting off from Grasmere in
1941 are typical youth hostellers.*

HOLIDAYS IN THE COUNTRY

*This picture is captioned, 'Sir Harry and Lady Brittain
are at present spending an ideal holiday in a Flatavan on
the Dorset Coast, having travelled from London through
the New Forest, finally pitching at Lulworth Cove.' The
Caravan Club of Great Britain and Ireland was founded
in June 1907, 'to bring together those interested in van-life
as a pastime'; the annual subscription was 5 shillings.
It took some time for members to admit that the future of
caravanning lay with the motor car and trailer, rather
than the horse-drawn waggon. Although Bank Holidays
were introduced in 1871 it was not until 1938 that
paid holidays became law. Both bicycling and hiking
were favourite occupations.*

HOP-PICKERS' HOLIDAYS

*East End children enjoy fresh air and sunshine in
Bodiam in 1951: three of the 40,000 or so
Londoners who went hop-picking in Kent and
Sussex every September. Behind are the long rows of
corrugated iron sheds that were their sleeping
quarters. In the evenings there were camp fires,
dancing and impromptu concerts. Another group
have their photograph taken on the last night. This
traditional holiday for townsfolk dates back to the
1860s. Groups also went picking the fruit in
Herefordshire and Worcestershire.*

E X P L O R I N G   T H E
C O U N T R Y S I D E

*Motorists admire the beauties of the
countryside between the wars, a pleasure for
the privileged few. At this time the cheapest
new car cost £117 10s, and 22 out of the 25
million population earned less than £250
per year. After the Second World War petrol
rationing lasted until 1950; hence the huge
popularity of cycle clubs. Members of this
London club, whizzing through a Surrey
village in June 1948, were planning a 60-
mile round trip.*

EXPLORING OTHER LIFESTYLES

Charabanc outings were a popular feature of post-war life. Here, a group – all in their Sunday best – visit Longleat in Wiltshire in 1953. The Marquess of Bath was the first to open his stately home to the general public, which he did in 1949. The increasing difficulty of maintaining large country houses like Longleat led to the transfer of many others to the National Trust in the 1950s and 1960s, and for country house visiting to become a national hobby. Meanwhile, some English holidaymakers explore no other way of life than that of tent and caravan in Dawlish.

THE BRANCH LINE

*The impact of the railway on English country life is hard to
imagine, changing as it did almost every aspect of people's lives.
By 1912 there was a rail network of 23,000 miles, allowing
people and goods to travel long distances in a relatively short
time. Apart from a few isolated areas, notably in Dorset and
Northumberland, most people were within fairly easy reach of a
station. A typical rural railway station (above) was at Ashley on
the Isle of Wight, photographed in 1923. Some large country
houses had their own private stations, such as Avon Lodge in
Hampshire, where a weekend visitor might alight for Avon
Castle. The railway also made a dramatic difference to the
marketing of perishable goods: here strawberries are being loaded
onto a train bound for London in 1922.*

THE MARKET TOWN

*For the majority of people living in the
country in the 19th century, and on into the
middle of the next, their travels were unlikely
to have taken them further than their local
market town. The market town was the
centre for all important transactions, local
trade and manufacture, local professional
practices and, of course, the markets
themselves. The ancient cobbled market
square of Richmond in Yorkshire is
shown almost empty of life – perhaps on
a Sunday – in contrast to the bustle of a
livestock market in the main streets of
Aylesbury in Buckinghamshire in 1912.*

THE MARKET

Shipston-on-Stour in Warwickshire in about 1905. The annual Christmas fatstock show is in progress in the main street. This was at a time when cattle would have been driven to market and before marketplaces were established on the outskirts of towns, close to the railway station and with space for trailers and lorries. It was reckoned that cattle could not be driven at faster than 2 miles an hour; even so, in the 19th century they were regularly driven from the Midlands and East Anglia to the London markets, where they fetched the best prices. The turnpike at Brandon in Suffolk recorded 8,000 cattle and 46,500 sheep passing through in 1845.

CHRISTMAS FAT STOCK SHOW.
SHIPSTON·ON·STOUR. SB87.

THE MARKET

*Most markets and fairs were medieval in origin and were
established by royal charter, although from the 1840s
onwards they came increasingly under the control of the
local authorities. Many markets were founded specifically
for one type of product or produce, or species of livestock –
butter, wool, sheep, geese. However, all towns had a
general market as well, selling locally-produced goods and
also cheap manufactured items. This for many people was
their principal opportunity to shop. Market day (above)
in Helmsley, Yorkshire, and (right) an elderly lady
appraises the draper's stall in a Cambridge market in
1938.*

TOWNSCAPES

The medieval Buttercross in Chichester (left), the original site of the butter market and always a popular spot to congregate. The High Street in Guildford (right), with the shops that would have been a magnet for the well-to-do for miles around. For towns such as Colchester the river was an important line of communication (below); here a barge is being loaded from a mill.

THE AUCTION

*The traditional way of disposing of
land, livestock or, in this case (right),
standing timber: an auction sale taking
place in 1933 on the bowling green of
the Shrewsbury Arms, at Rugeley in
Staffordshire. The sale was billed as
being of half a million cubic feet of
'magnificent growing British timber'
from the estate of 'the late Lord
Bagot'. Forthcoming attractions could
be seen posted up on the wall.
The sale (above) of fatstock at the
Home Farm, Windsor.*

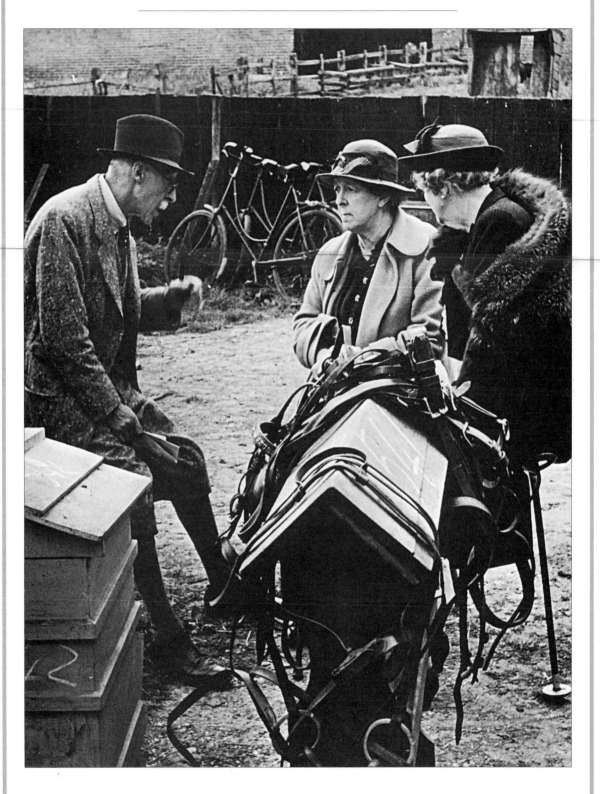

THE COUNTRY HOUSE SALE

The Depression and the Second War led to the sale of many large country houses and the dispersal of their contents. (It was at this time that the National Trust started to extend its powers of preservation from land to country houses.) The sales were unmissable local events, providing everyone with a chance to meet, have a gossip and perhaps reminisce about the past.

ANIMAL FAIRS

Horse and pony fairs, such as those held annually at Appleby in Yorkshire and Barnet in Hertfordshire, saw huge crowds of horse copers, who travelled miles to make a deal. A horse being shown off at Barnet Horse Fair (left) in 1926. Queen Elizabeth I granted the charter for this fair in 1588. Prior to their sale the animals would be grazed on Barnet Common. A scene at Bampton in Devon (above), at the annual round-up and sale of Exmoor ponies.

THE AGRICULTURAL SHOW

The high point of the farmer's year, and a chance to see the latest agricultural machinery on display. This picture shows the Massey-Harris stand at the Bath and West Show in 1921. The most important agricultural show was the one organized by the Royal Agricultural Society, which was staged annually from 1839. Competition for the farmers' custom among the different manufacturers of agricultural implements and machinery was fierce. The Royal Society arranged trials and ploughing matches between the different companies.

COMPETITION

*Dorset Horn lambs (far left)
await the verdict of the judges at
a farm show in Dorchester in
the summer of 1949. The
Mayor of Plymouth (above)
views the poultry at the West of
England Show in 1925. In the
autumn of 1946 at Stoke Chew
in Somerset (left), a barrow-
load of giant cabbages is
wheeled in to compete.*

THE SUMMER FÊTE

*'If wet in the village hall': despite the vagaries
of English summer weather, the fête was a
permanent fixture in the country calendar, and
all in a good cause. An entertainment by the
Shoreham Village Players in 1925 (above), at a
fête held at Somerhill, near Tonbridge (the seat
of Colonel Davigdor Goldsmid – as the picture
announces), in aid of the Queen Alexandra
Nurses Fund. Scene on the vicarage lawn at
Chislet in Kent (left), just a week before the
outbreak of war in 1939*

AT THE RACES

Two views of racing: the Ladies taking the first jump, side-saddle, at the Berks and Bucks Farmers point-to-point meeting in 1927 (above), and the pit pony 'Barger' coming in first at the Pit Pony Derby held at Thorpe near Wakefield (above left). The jockeys in the paddock (left and right).

THE SPORTING CALENDAR

*Correct attire to the smallest detail was de rigeur for all
sporting events, as shown by these pictures from the
'Twenties and 'Thirties.*

THE FAIR COMES TO TOWN

*A view of Pinner in Middlesex on the day of its annual
fair in 1936, exactly 600 years after the town had been
granted its charter by King John. The charter allowed for
a market to be held every Wednesday, and for two fairs
every year. Only one fair survived, on the first Wednesday
after Whitsun. Important components of fairs were the
merry-go-rounds, with their magnificently carved, painted
and gilded figures and animals, such as the ones being set
up for Mitcham fair in the 1930s.*

THE FAIR COMES TO TOWN

*The traditional joys of the roundabout at
Beaconsfield in 1922. The steam-powered
roundabout, with accompanying organ music,
made its appearance in the 1860s, the invention
of Frederick Savage of King's Lynn, who
devised it as a sideline to his agricultural
machinery business.*